I recently had a conversation with an old friend of mine. We got to talking about all of our critters from way back when. Youth I suppose. He said that he was an animal person, as I was too. I brought up my owl story after which he said that I should put it down on paper. Well, as I am some just six months from turning 80 years old; being not that much time left, and while I can still remember, I thought it over and decided I'd give it a try as I have never written anything much, other than letters and such. Hope you like it···it was good while I lived it.

The story starts in the fall of 1946 I believe, and it starts with my horse. I lived on a dairy farm in the Midwest. When I started high school, "1946". If you lived on a dairy farm, you took four years of agriculture whether you wanted too or not. The second year our project was to lay out a plan, go to the bank with the class, and borrow money from the bank, then buy what was called "fat stock".

Well we went to the bank as a group, worked out our loan, then, on another trip we went to South St. Paul, Minnesota, to the stockyards. It was rather big in those days. Cattle came in by the trainload. Most of the class bought beef cattle.

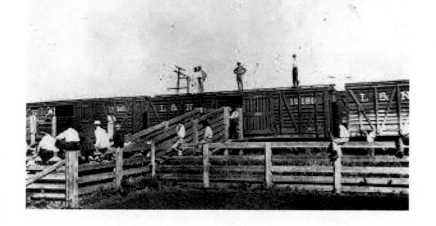

Now, I really don't like dairy cows. I like the red ones with the white faces, and the calves to the milking. My father really never understood that about me.

With my limited funds I bought eight sheep.

Well I took my sheep home and fatten them up. Kept good records on the cost of the feed, etc. when they were fat enough, then I shipped them back to the stockyards in South St. Paul, Minnesota. Sold them and made some money.

But I kept one, as sheep go, he was a nice one. That one I took up to the northwest fat livestock show in the Midwest. Would you believe, I won first place in my class. After the show, all animals were sold at auction. To the big meatpackers, restaurants and such. I made more money on that one sheep than what I did on all the others. Went home, paid the bank off; that was a good feeling, and then turned in my paperwork to school. Got a good grade too. Well now, I had money in my pocket.

Every Saturday when I could, I got a job at a local cattle auction. Made $5.00 a day and the free coffee.

Don't worry we'll get to the owl a little later.

This one Saturday a skinny colt showed up for sale. I always wanted a saddle horse, but could never afford one. This colt was ill kept and hungry looking. Every time you walked by him back would go his ears. Didn't seem to like anything or anybody for that matter, well you know, I just couldn't help myself. I bought him for $12.50, if I remember right.

Got a truck to haul it home for me. It took four men to get him loaded and seven men with ropes to get him unloaded and into the barn. He spent most of the winter in the box stall.

Taming the horse was much easier than getting my father to let me keep him. But, by early summer I was on his back. He seemed to get along with me, seemed to do whatever I wanted him to do, and enjoyed doing it. The horse got fat and I was happy. I had a little saddle horse. Best of all, my dad let me keep him.

Now, onto the rest of the story.

We left the farm, which didn' t seem to
bother me too much. No more milk cows.

We were located on a small place just
outside the small town of about 400
people. Maybe that' s stretching it a bit
by a hundred people.

We had a small home on about six acres of pasture, so I could take my horse along.

One weekend I went down to spend the weekend with my aunt and uncle. Maybe to do some fishing. They lived alongside this nice trout stream. It was more of a coolie than a valley. The first day there, I went down river where I knew of a nice hole, just below some 50 foot cliffs.

While fishing, I thought I'd seen
something flopping around at the base of
the cliff.

So I went back upstream a ways where the water wasn't so deep. I crossed over and went back down to the base of the cliff.

There was a little owl crawling around. Must of fell out of the nest way up the cliff. No way for me to get up there, and I knew he couldn't last long here on the ground.

We had a lot of critters that would have loved to eat him come nightfall. So he became mine I guess. He wasn't even old enough to have pinfeathers, just fuzz.

When I got him back to my uncle's house, they all told me that it wouldn't make it so I should go out and do away with him. Now you know I couldn't do that with him. So I set about trying to feed him. Now not being Mama Owl, I wasn't just too sure how to do that. So I learned at an early age. If it don't fit, force it.

I liberated hamburger out of the house, took that out to the shop, pried his beak open and shoved some hamburger in. That went down OK, didn't have too much trouble with the second load, and by the third try he seen it coming and opened up on his own. The rest of the day I spent down on the river catching little fish, frogs and whatever I thought he might eat. From that day on there was no end to the amount that bird could eat.

When I got home on Sunday night with a box under my arm, I was met at the door. "What have you brought home this time?" Well I had been through this many times before, so it took a while to explain. That owl ended up in the box under the sink in the kitchen. It took about a week for them to warm up to him.

One day my mother asked me, "What's his name?" Don't know just how, but I opened my mouth and out came, "Screw Dinkle".

And it stuck. Screw Dinkle was his name.

The word went out around the village that an owl lived at our house. We did get a lot of visitors. I made a deal with all the little kids around. If they would bring the small fish, frogs and meat scraps, I would let them watch me feed him. Worked too. And some of the local butchers heard about the owl and they would drive in the yard with a big package of trimmings. So he was never without food. As I said before, he liked to eat.

As he grew and grew, he feathered out, I discovered that he was a Great Horned Owl. At this full growth he was about 3" to 4" bigger than the normal size for them than the normal Great Horned Owls. They have two groups of big feathers on their head that look like big ears. At full growth, he was a very large bird, and he out grew about four boxes under the sink. That was home I guess.

When he was all feathered out and could begin to fly he learned that on his own.

I didn' t teach him that, I didn' t know how to fly until I was 21 and got my license, always thought of him when I was flying.

After he grew and could fly, after we had breakfast, and he had his morning feed. He would sit on the floor and wait till we ate, then he would get his. Then he would walk or hop to the door ready to go outside but first I must tell you about his night.

Around dinner time, you would hear him at the door. A little squawk, then if you did not open it, he would peck at the door a few times, he would then sit on the floor by his box and wait for dinner scraps. He seemed to know that he would get some. Then later in the evening, he would spend about an hour chasing the squares on the kitchen floor. That was fun to watch.

Then when it was time to go to bed, we would start to turn out the lights, we would say, "It' s bedtime Screw Dinkle", he would hop right into his box, and stay there all night.

But the first time I would turn over in bed in the morning that meant it was time to get up. Here he would come, hopping up the stairs and screeching at every step. Come right over to my bed and stand there looking at me with those big eyes.

When I got to the stairs, down he would fly, land on the kitchen floor and slide all the way across the floor and bang up against the door. Before he started flying, he used to hop down the stairs and usually end up tumbling down the last few.

I suppose he was happy when he learned to fly. Then he would sit quietly while we were at breakfast. Then he got his and it was time to go outside; always had frogs and fish in the bucket on the porch that the kids would bring, then he would get some of them and was off doing whatever he did every day.

He would do a morning flyby, or whatever you call it. Sometimes he would be gone for a half a day at a time. At first I was a little worried that maybe he would leave. But after a while I didn't think much about it. He usually would show up when you called him. He did spend some time in the little barn we had, hunting mice I suppose. We had some chickens and ducks and he seemed to get along with them OK. He didn't mind and they didn't either.

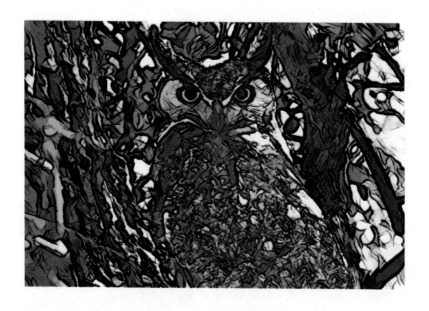

We had an evergreen tree in the yard, not to sure just what kind it was, but it was sort of fancy. It was very full, you couldn' t see into it, but the owl figured it out.

Now please remember owls and crows are lifetime enemies. Owls hunt crows at night, and crows hunt owls in the daytime.

The first time I had seen this happen I wasn't just too sure what was going on. The owl was running around the tree screeching as loud as he could. Soon here comes the crows and Screw Dinkle would run under the tree, then run up the tree; he would go limb to limb. About halfway up you would see his head poke out, screech and duck back in. Soon he would appear farther up and do the same thing. This would go on for some time after a while the crows would give up and fly away.

He would then come down, flying out to the barn to hunt mice or whatever he did out there. There were a few times that he would go on one of these fly-abouts. Where that was, I never knew. Once in a while you could hear some screeching and crows making noise and here he would come, heading for the tree in the yard and go through the whole thing all over again. There were a few times when I was outside, I would call him with the door to the house open. But he had that tree all figured out. That was his world I guess besides I really do think that he enjoyed the whole thing and he was doing it on purpose.

In the afternoon when I didn' t have some kind of a job I would come home and whistle to my horse who always came to go for a ride. Now I didn' t have a saddle or a real bridle, but I have taught the horse to feel my knees and that' s how I steered him.

Just for fun I would ride down to the village and ride around for a bit. Looking at it now I suppose I was just showing off a bit. There was a bar down there and when I would ride up on the sidewalk in front of the bar; yes they did have sidewalks, not many though. Anyway, the bartender would bring me out a grape pop. "Sort of like the stuff." Now, please remember this was right after the Second World War and where I lived times were not all that good for some people. My family was among those I guess. So, even though the pop cost only 5 cents, I didn' t always have spare change in my pocket, so I made that trip at least twice a week. A pop was a pop, especially when it was free. I always looked at it as some kind of a show. I earned it, oats wasn' t free neither you know.

There were some big farmers, at that time, who had done quite well during the war. There were a few who had spent a few bucks on fancy saddle horses. Well, when they came into town to do their thing they went over to the bar for an afternoon of beer. They would come out and watch me and mine. No saddle, bridle, just bare back. The horse would stop, go, turn and back up. It bothered them a bit I think. There were a few who watched and would say, "Kid shouldn' t be riding around town on that horse with no way to control him." But the guy who owned the bar would just bring me out another pop and tell the old boys they should hire me to train their horses. Bless that bartender, but that never came to pass. I guess they didn' t want to part with their money. Oh well, that' s the way it was then.

But, let's go back to Screw Dinkle. He and the horse seemed to get along, sorta I guess. The owl used to spend time walking around the pasture, looking for mice I suppose. The horse never seemed to bother him much, but one day when I was watching, the horse walked over and put his head down to smell Screw Dinkle, I guess. Well when the nose came in reach, the owl reached up with one of those big feet he had and grabbed the horse by the nose. The horse squealed and took off. The owl still with him, the horse cleared the gate by at least one foot. He had long legs you know. I didn't even know he could jump. Down the driveway he went, which hits the main road to town. I was told later that he had made several trips around town.

Then he came home and cleared the gate again. When his feet hit the ground the owl let go. He was home again. Instead of heading for the barn; the poor horse stayed in the far end of the pasture and wouldn't come when I called him. I had to lead him back to the barn and doctor up the holes in his nose. He never tried to smell the owl again. The horse would never come near the owl again unless I was around.

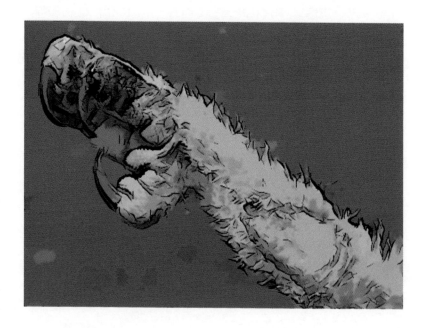

I have never picked up the owl, only when he was little, however there came a day. I thought, "Just how am I going to do this?" He had huge talons on his feet, so one day I got a bunch of what we called gunny sacks. I am told that they are now called burlap bags. I still like gunny sacks though, maybe because I'm getting old, who knows. So I started wrapping my arm in gunny sacks, got the owl on my arm, with food of course. Got to where I could call him and he would fly up and land on my arm. One day as I was going to go for a ride, I decided to see if the owl would ride on my arm on horseback. "Well, it worked." Got on the horse, called the owl, and here he came, landed on my arm and didn't dig in too deep. The horse of course was a little worried, but away we went. I do think that the owl enjoyed it because we were up in the air a bit and it let him see around.

When he would see me with my arm wrapped, he was right there. When I got on my horse he would fly right up and land on my arm. One day I rode out into the field, a pheasant flew up and the owl was off my arm like a shot.

Caught the pheasant in midair, then brought it back to me. Well, I was excited about that. We had a new game and food on the table.

We went back to the barn, gave the horse a handful of oats. Looked around and the owl was sitting next to the pheasant. I went over and skinned the bird and cleaned it out to take to the house. The owl took care of the leavings. So I wonder if that would work again. The next day we did the same thing. The pheasant would come up and then the owl was off and came back with the bird. Came home with three birds one night. We ate a lot of pheasants that summer. After all the pheasant leavings he was always back at the door at night. Had his dinner and in his box he went.

I think what I'm trying to say is that Screw Dinkle was free. I think that it is important. He lived in our house because he wanted to. Not because he had to live in a cage. I don't like cages - wouldn't want to live in one myself. He came home every night, stayed in his box under the sink and was up in the morning, even though he was a night bird. Maybe because he never had mama owl to teach him what owls were supposed to do. But he seemed to do OK.

There was another thing he used to do. Most of the farm houses in that area had basements and they always seemed to have mice and rat problems. Well, Screw Dinkle and I worked that out too. I rented him out for 50 cents a night to live in basements. He never seemed to mind. Didn' t seem to bother him at all. I would take him out to a farm, take him down in the basement and leave a dish of water, then close the door, I would tell the farmer not to go down there for at least two days. Two days always seemed enough, he always seemed to be glad to see me, never mad. Would always have my arm wrapped in gunny sacks. Riding in the car never seemed to bother him at all. In fact I think he liked it, sort of enjoyed looking out the window. When we got home he would fly around a bit, then land at the door to the house ready to eat. Eat he did. But I had good reports from the farmers that they had no more mice problems. I even got a dollar tip a few times.

But he was free, as I get older and think back, it was so nice to have a relationship with a bird that was free. Not just a pet; a pet I think he was not. He was just free. He lived at my house because he wanted to, part of the family I guess. And speaking of family, after that they'd meet me at the door saying, "What did you bring home now?" They accepted him too. And I am sure they enjoyed him as much as I did. In fact I know they did, as did all the little kids who spent their days catching frogs and fish, just to watch me feed him.

I do remember, only one time, I rode downtown to the bar with the bird on my arm. The bar owner came out with a pop for me and a piece of jerky for the owl, then one for the horse. He liked jerky too. There was a bit of a crowd that day. It was a different life then. Times were different too.

The rest of the story must come next. As you grow older, you must go out into the world and start to make, as my father told me, "Make a living". I had finished school, no way for me to make a living where I lived. I certainly was not going to get a job on a farm milking cows. So, I went up to "the city", as they called it where I came from. I went to St. Paul, Minnesota and got a job. It was not what I wanted, and not where I wanted to be so my father said, "The horse must go".

There was some family friends who had two small girls who wanted a horse. While I was gone their father came down, put a bridle on the horse, which he had brought with him. Got on the horse to see how he rode. They went about 30 feet and the horse popped him off and broke his collar bone. My father told him that no one had ever rode him before, other than me. The man bought him anyway and took him home.

A week later, I came home for the weekend and went out to see them and the horse. I believe he was glad to see me. I rode him around a little bit and then put the girls on him. Walked him around a bit and it all worked out. They rode him until he grew old and passed on I was told. But the man who bought him for his girls was never able to ride him.

I got tired of the winter snow, cold weather and such so I said goodbye to Screw Dinkle and moved to the West Coast, Puget Sound. Got there in early January and can you believe it? It was green. I learned later why it was green in January – "rain". It was what I wanted with mountains close by if you want snow. You could drive up to it and then come home to the mild. And in the summer it was a good place to go camping. After about a year I went back and brought my parents out. Not much back there for them. After I brought my folks out here the Korean War was on and I had to go.

Now the story of Screw Dinkle was somewhat different. Before my folks came out here my dad found an old lady who had a big farm. Her husband had passed, so she leased the farmland out. But, she too was an animal person. She had all kinds of critters. Even an old lion, who was missing most of his teeth. She rescued him from a circus. She was happy to get Screw Dinkle. She had some kind of a stand out at the end of her driveway with a sign that said, "Please do not put your arm out the window. The owl will ride on your hood if you drive slowly". When the car got up to the house, Screw Dinkle would get a treat and fly back to his stand to wait for the next car to come in. the odd thing about this was that he was still a day bird and he was still free. Like I said earlier, when I was flying, I always thought of Screw Dinkle, the Great Horned Owl, who remained free.

You know, I still miss my horse and the owl, even after all these years.

Author

Bill Olson

At a snow covered dairy farm in western Wisconsin on the first day of December 1932 my Grand Mother helped deliver me into this world.

Two hours later a doctor arrived in a horse drawn cutter sleigh moments ahead of a winter storm. After examining my mother and me he set out to return the fourteen miles back to town. Struggling through the blinding snow he had a heart attack and died never to register my birth.

I finished high school in 1950 at age 17, left the farm, and went to work at a hardware store in St. Paul, Minnesota for a while before heading out west.

When the Korean War broke out I enlisted in the Navy. After my enlistment I came home and have lived a good life; learned to fly, traveled, and other things. My ability to obtain a travel passport was complicated by the lack of a birth record, but it was eventually worked out.

By the way, the horses name was Rusty. Over the years I had three horses named Rusty. In remembrance of the first one I guess.

50152932R00027

Made in the USA
Charleston, SC
15 December 2015